ShowTime® Piano

Kids' Songs

2011 EDITION

Level 2A

Elementary Playing

This book belongs to: _____

T0057143

Arranged by

Nancy and Randall Faber

Production Coordinator: Jon Ophoff
Design and Illustration: Terpstra Design, San Francisco
Engraving: Dovetree Productions, Inc.

FABER
PIANO ADVENTURES®

3042 Creek Drive
Ann Arbor, Michigan 48108

A NOTE TO TEACHERS

ShowTime® Piano Kids' Songs is a collection of popular songs that brings special joy to children. The variety, humor, and charm of the selections is especially engaging for the elementary pianist.

The book is graded 2A and is specifically written to provide a smooth transition for the student between Level 1 and Level 2. Pieces are in the keys of C, G, F, A minor, and D minor, and begin gradually moving the hands outside of the 5-finger position. Circled finger numbers help alert the student to a change of hand position. Melodies are harmonized simply, usually with single notes or harmonic intervals.

ShowTime® Piano Kids' Songs is part of the *ShowTime® Piano* series. "ShowTime" designates Level 2A of the *PreTime® to BigTime® Piano Supplementary Library* arranged by Faber and Faber.

Following are the levels of the supplementary library, which lead from *PreTime®* to *BigTime®*.

PreTime® Piano	(Primer Level)
PlayTime® Piano	(Level 1)
ShowTime® Piano	(Level 2A)
ChordTime® Piano	(Level 2B)
FunTime® Piano	(Level 3A – 3B)
BigTime® Piano	(Level 4)

Each level offers books in a variety of styles, making it possible for the teacher to offer stimulating material for every student. For a complimentary detailed listing, e-mail faber@pianoadventures.com or write us at the mailing address below.

Visit **www.PianoAdventures.com**.

Helpful Hints:

1. Rhythmic continuity can be improved by having the student tap the piece, hands together. (Use the palm or fingertips on the closed fallboard.)

2. Key signatures are not used until late in the *ShowTime®* level. Where key signatures are used, one-octave scales (hands alone) can help orient the student to the piece.

3. Singing the words to *ShowTime® Kids' Songs* can add to the enjoyment and helps the student grasp phrasing and rhythm.

ISBN 978-1-61677-040-2

TABLE OF CONTENTS

Chim Chim Cher-ee

From Walt Disney's *Mary Poppins*

Words and Music by
RICHARD M. SHERMAN
and ROBERT B. SHERMAN

Cheerfully, lightly

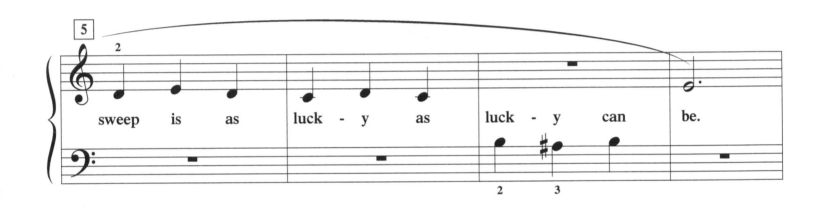

Teacher Duet: (Student plays 1 octave higher)

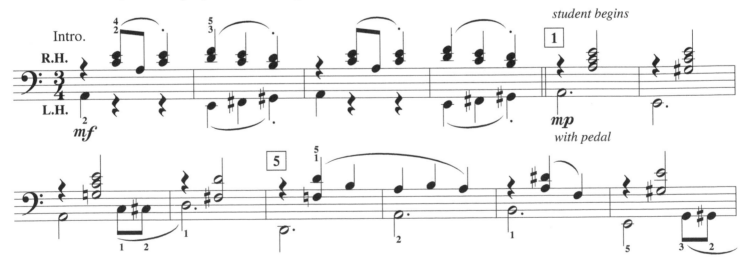

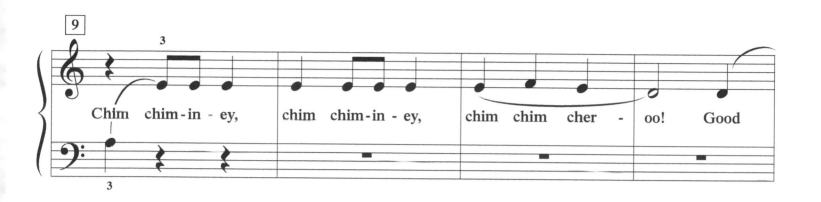

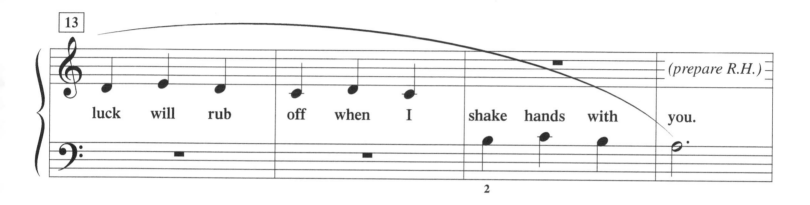

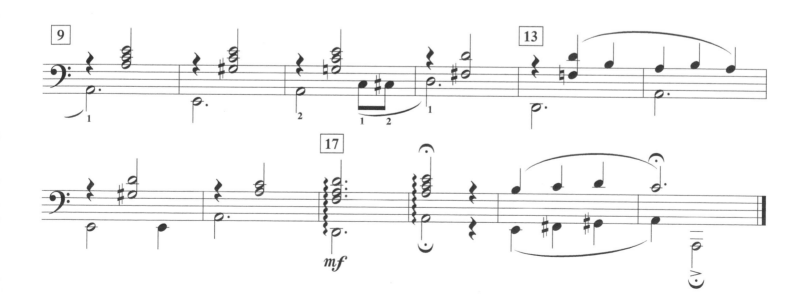

Tomorrow

From the Musical Production *Annie*

Lyric by
MARTIN CHARNIN

Music by
CHARLES STROUSE

Teacher Duet: (Student plays 1 octave higher)

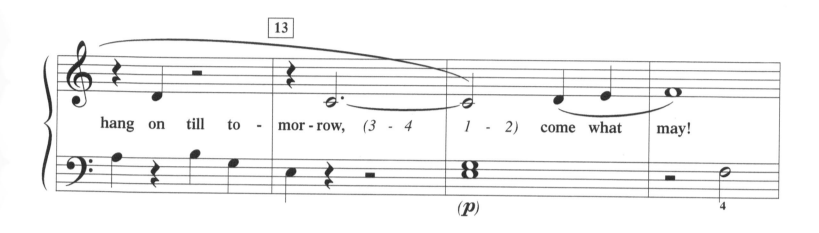

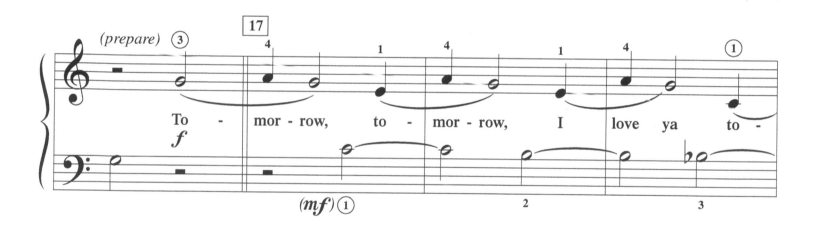

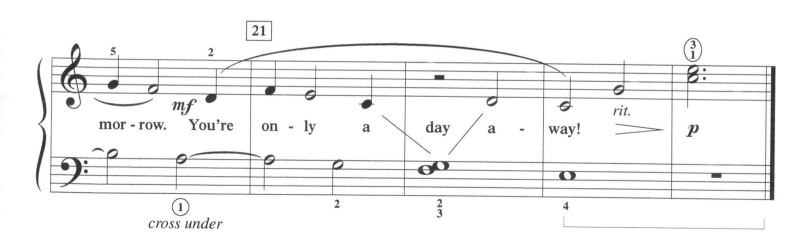

Mail Myself to You

Words and Music by
WOODY GUTHRIE

Cheerfully

I'm gonna wrap my - self in pa - per, I'm gonna daub my - self with glue.

Teacher Duet: (Student plays 1 octave higher)

Stick some stamps on top (of) my head, I'm gonna mail my - self to you.

f

L.H. ② over

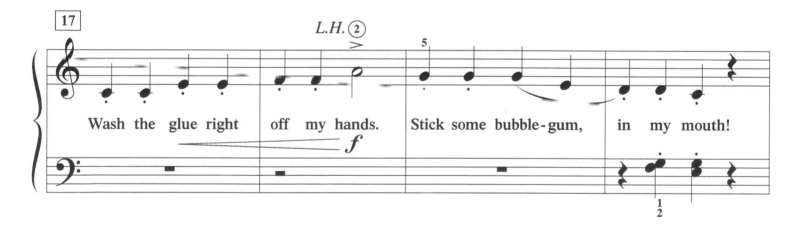

When you see me in your mail - box, cut the string and let me out.

p

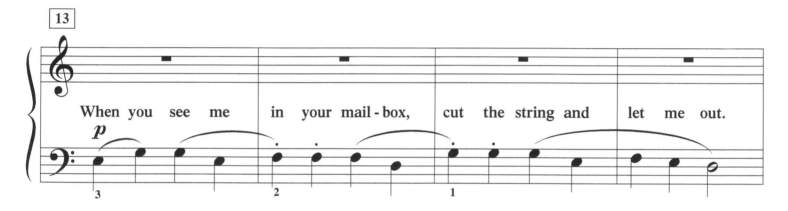

Wash the glue right off my hands. Stick some bubble-gum, in my mouth!

f

L.H. ②

stick some bubble-gum in my mouth!

p   *f*

The Hokey Pokey

Words and Music by
CHARLES P. MACAK, TAFFT BAKER,
and LARRY LaPRISE

Moderately, with a swing*

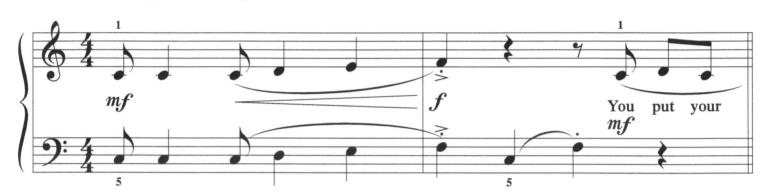

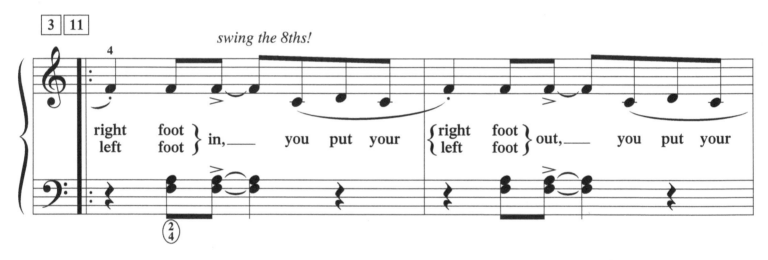

*Note to Teacher: ♫ should be played in a long-short pattern (♫ = 𝅘𝅥𝅮³𝅘𝅥𝅮).

Teacher Duet: (Student plays 1 octave higher)

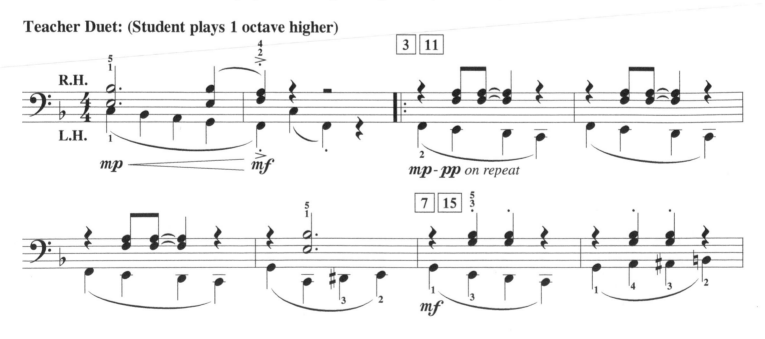

right foot
left foot } in,___ and you shake it all a - bout.

7 15

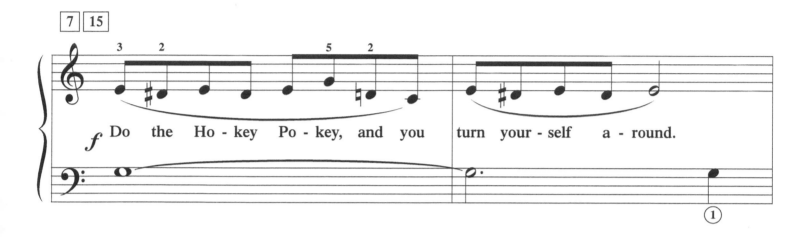

Do the Ho - key Po - key, and you turn your - self a - round.

That's what it's all a - bout. You put your bout.

The Pirates Who Don't Do Anything

From *VeggieTales*

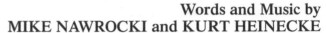

Words and Music by
MIKE NAWROCKI and KURT HEINECKE

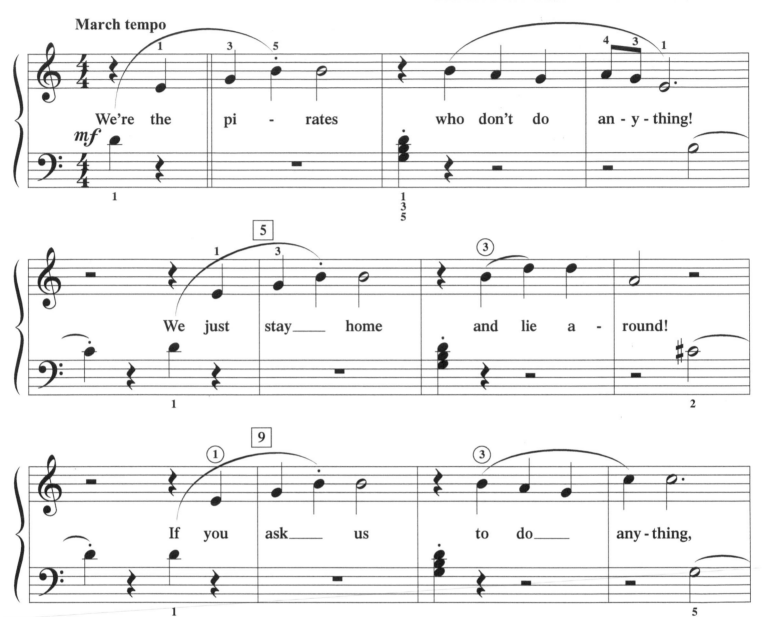

Teacher Duet: (Student plays 1 octave higher)

What Do Witches Eat?

Lyrics by JENNIFER MacLEAN
Music by NANCY FABER

*Note to Teacher: ♫ should be played in a long-short pattern (♫ = $\overline{3}$ ♪).

Teacher Duet: (Student plays 1 octave higher)

Bling-Blang (Build a House)

Words and Music by
WOODY GUTHRIE

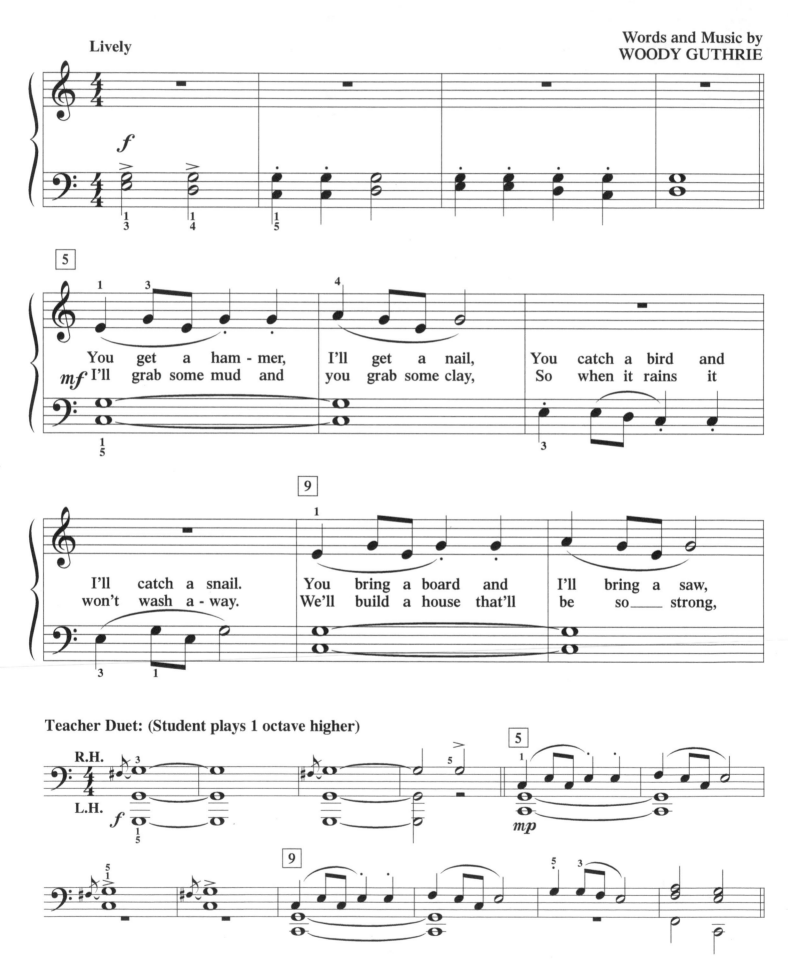

Shaggy Dog Bop

Words and Music by
NANCY FABER

Strutting along proudly

My hair's so long, ba - by,
strut so fine and my
I__ can't see,
ears__ are cool, } I'm the
Sha - Sha - Sha -

Shag - gy Dog. { I
I like my looks, ba - by,
e - ven went to a
I__ love me,
ca - nine school, } I'm the

Sha - Sha - Sha -
Shag - gy Dog. { When I
I go out on the
like the mail - man, he

Teacher Duet: (Student plays 1 octave higher)

R.H.

L.H.

legato

Jig Along Home

Quickly, with spirit

Words and Music by
WOODY GUTHRIE

Teacher Duet: (Student plays 1 octave higher)

jig a - long home. Jig, jig, jig, jig, jig 'long home,

jig, jig, jig, jig, jig a - long home. Jig, jig, jig a - long,

jig 'long home. Jig a - long, jig a - long, jig a - long home.

8va _ _ _ (Omit for duet)

Oompa-Loompa Doompadee-Doo

From WILLY WONKA AND THE CHOCOLATE FACTORY

Words and Music by
LESLIE BRICUSSE
and ANTHONY NEWLEY

Teacher Duet: (Student plays 1 octave higher)

24

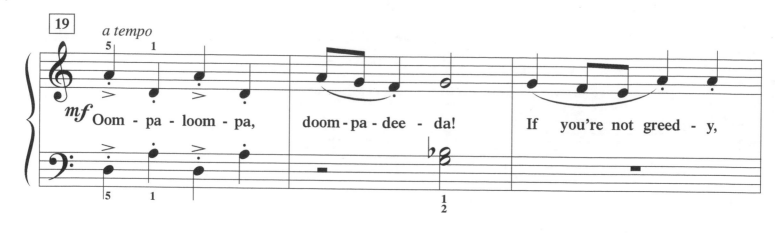

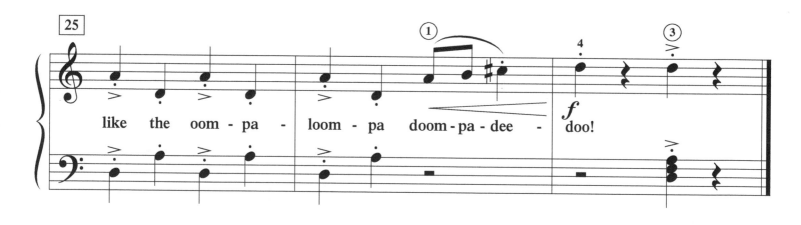